THE BOOK
of
BELLE VUE

THE BOOK
of
BELLE VUE

STEVE UTTLEY & TONY BLUFF

STADIA

This book is dedicated to the many thousands of Rovers fans who spent their Saturday afternoons shouting their team on at their beloved Belle Vue.

First published 2005
Reprinted 2007

STADIA is an imprint of
Tempus Publishing Limited
Cirencester Road, Chalford,
Stroud, Gloucestershire, GL6 8PE
www.tempus-publishing.com

British Library Cataloguing in Publication Data.
A catalogue record for this book is available from the British Library.

ISBN-10: 0 7524 3056 4
ISBN-13: 978 0 7524 3056 0

Typesetting and origination by Tempus Publishing Limited.
Printed in Great Britain.

Contents

Programme seller Mr Wheatley stands in his usual spot.

Acknowledgements

Special thanks to John Ryan, Joe Hoggins, Ian McMahon, Barry Watson, Joan Oldale, Stuart Highfield, David Morris, Peter White and Chas Walker.

Introduction

At the AGM of the Rovers in June 1902 a call was made for an approach to be made to the Doncaster Corporation for some land to be made available for a new ground for the club. This was in response to the uncertainty regarding the tenancy of the Intake ground. The Corporation selected a special committee to find a suitable site and, at a meeting in August 1902, this committee recommended that the club should be offered, on a yearly tenancy or lease at £2 per acre per annum, about six acres of the Low Pastures. The site was on the other side of the Great North Road opposite to the racecourse and was open scrub land. The recommendation came, though, with a sting in the tail. A condition of accepting the site would mean agreeing not to erect any wooden stands that would obstruct the view across the Pastures from the Great North Road. Councillor Wightman accused the Race Committee of erecting stands that blocked the view of the common and here they were wanting to restrict the football club from possibly doing the same. The Rovers committee turned the offer down because of the restriction on the size of any stands.

In May 1920, upon the re-formation of the club, the Corporation were once again asked for a suitable site for them to play on as their old ground at the Intake was not available. The following month, a deputation from the club met the Estates Committee of the Corporation and were taken to see the proposed site, a six-acre area on the Low Pastures opposite the racecourse. The deputation's recommendation to accept the site was accepted by the club but it would need time to build a suitable ground on what was then scrub land. The Corporation offered the use of the Education Committee's playing fields at Belle Vue, Bennetthorpe, now covered by Nuttall's Cottages.

Meanwhile the work began on the new ground at the Low Pastures. The levelling of the ground was done by removing 500 loads of earth and dumping 50,000 loads of ash to form the foundation of the pitch and the banking surrounding it. A main stand was built to seat 4,000 people and terracing in front of the stand held 3,000.

The ground was opened on Saturday 26 August 1922 by Mr Charles E. Sutcliffe of the Management Committee of the Football League. Various other VIP guests were also present. The Doncaster Subscription Band played while Mr Sutcliffe was shown around the new ground. There were enormous queues at the turnstiles so it was decided to admit the public before the official opening ceremony. In his opening speech Mr Sutcliffe congratulated the club on having built an excellent ground and thought the pitch would be wonderful to play on. After the opening ceremony had been performed the Midland League match against Gainsborough Trinity was played in front of a crowd of 10,000, a record attendance to watch a football game in Doncaster. The score was 0-0.

Although always known as the Low Pastures, it was decided that the name of Belle Vue would be transferred from the previous ground and that henceforth the new ground would be known as such. And so it has been.

Various improvements were made as detailed under the respective sections. In 1935 with Second Division football achieved, the club spent £182 on new turnstiles, fencing and gates and another £600 on extensions and other improvements. Then, during that first season in the Second Division (1935/36) they spent a further £287 on banking and terracing.

In September 1938 the club negotiated a new lease on the ground for a further twenty-one years. This was renegotiated in March 1950 for a lease of sixty years.

During the 1951/52 season the floodlights, used for training on dark nights, were upgraded to match standard by the installation of four towers with twelve lamps on each to cover the whole playing area. The cost of around £2,000 was recouped by playing attractive friendly games. Doncaster Rovers were actually the first club outside London, and the first in the North, to stage a floodlit match on 4 March 1952. That night 18,474 people turned out to see this new phenomenon when the Rovers met Hibernian in an entertaining game, won by the Scots. In 1965 new floodlights cost the club £15,000.

In the 1970s the capacity of the ground was cut to 21,150, including 2,010 seats. Then in 1985 came the Valley Parade fire and the Heysel Stadium disaster. This brought into force the Safety of Sports Grounds Act, reducing the capacity at a stroke to fewer than 10,000. Under the terms of this Act the Town End Stand was demolished and the Main Stand required fire-cladding and new exits from the stand to the terrace in front. Together with various other improvements costing a total of £450,000, seventy-five per cent of which was paid as a grant by the Football Grounds Improvement Trust, the capacity of the ground was put at 9,900. In 1987 the Popular Stand was taken down because of mining subsidence resulting in the capacity of the ground being reduced to 4,859. It was made into an open terrace and, with the Rossington End being extended for the away supporters in 1988, the capacity of the ground was raised to 8,259. Then came the Hillsborough Disaster in April 1989. All standing area limits were cut by fifteen per cent, thus reducing the capacity of the ground to 7,294.

In July 1995 an arson attack on the Main Stand caused £100,000 of damage, even though only a portion of the centre of the stand was damaged. This was cordoned off until remedial work could be carried out. The police investigations revealed that Ken Richardson, the Rovers owner, was the man who instigated the action carried out by a private investigator from Newcastle. In January 1999, Richardson was found guilty of conspiring to burn down the Main Stand and was jailed for four years.

In 1997 the club was told by the Football Licensing Authority that they would be refused a safety certificate unless a new toilet block was built on the Popular side and new terracing laid down in front of the Main Stand. This amounted to a cost of around £100,000. The work was completed in time for the new season to start.

In the summer of 2004, work started on building an office block and clubhouse outside the Town End of the ground. It was opened in November 2004 so the office staff can now operate in modern amenities facilities. The outside ground has also been tarmacked so that on wet days one is not paddling through puddles.

one

Outside
Belle Vue

The large piece of land outside the ground has always been an ash surface. In the early years it accommodated the large number of people trying to get into the ground without inconveniencing the road users. Post–Second World War, it made an ideal car park as cars became more available to the general public. It is also used on racing days for horse boxes and other vehicles. Unfortunately, the surface of the car park is constantly in need of repair as potholes appear with the constant wear and tear upon it. Many spectators have had the experience of dodging the puddles in their trek to the turnstiles.

The fans' first view of Belle Vue as they walk to the match, showing the Main Stand and car park. This photograph was taken on a wet December day in 2000, and shows the many puddles that fans had to negotiate to reach the turnstiles.

The back of the Main Stand as seen from the main road – this is often mistaken by non-locals for a commercial outlet. The advertising boards constitute an important revenue stream for the club.

The entrance to the club shop and the Supporters' Club in the Main Stand, summer 2001.

The turnstile for the terraces on the Main Stand: the results of a clean-up after a match await removal.

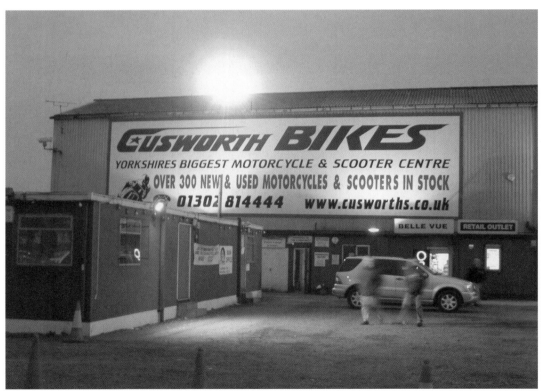

The new Cusworth advert gets its first showing at the Forest Green Rovers night game in October 2002.

Outside the Main Stand after arsonists set it on fire in July 1995. Note that there are no advertising hoardings on the stand.

The police stand guard on another wet night before the friendly game against Scunthorpe United on 7 August 2001.

A panoramic view of the Main Stand. It shows the portable cabin offices. The photograph was taken in January 2001.

Behind the Popular Stand terrace showing the Sky Television gantry first erected for the Dagenham & Redbridge game in September 2002.

Just in case the away fans get lost they are guided by this old sign attached to the wall outside the Town End.

two

Inside the
Main Stand

The Main Stand, built in 1922, seated 4,000 people and had terracing in front of it to hold another 3,000 spectators. In the summer of 1927, with funds provided by the Supporters' Club, the stand was extended to hold a total of 6,000 people. This extension was opened by the secretary of the FA on 27 August 1927 before the match against Lincoln City.

In 1985, under the terms of the Safety of Sports Grounds Act, this stand, being a wooden structure, had over £100,000 spent on fire-cladding and exit gates attached to the terrace in front of the stand. All smoking was banned to cohere with the Act, and emergency lighting and a new PA system were also installed. Following the Hillsborough Disaster in April 1989 the seating capacity was reduced to 1,259.

The kit man Dave Richards puts the shirts out in the home dressing room before a game. The kit man has to wait until the manager tells the team members whether they are playing before he knows which shirts to put out. This is often only an hour before the game.

Inside the players' entrance, this sign greets all who enter and directs them to where they should be. This is all most fans see of inside the Main Stand.

The home team's changing rooms and showers.

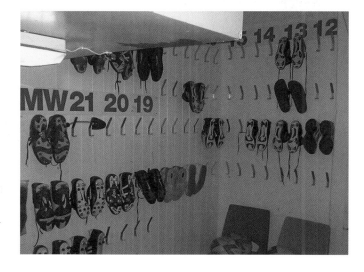

The boot room. Many young players have cleaned the boots of the first team here, but now players keep their own boots at home.

The main passage in the Main Stand. On the left-hand wall is the railway engine replica nameplate from the LNER locomotive. The original was sold during the early 1990s to raise funds for the club as it entered the dark era of the club's history.

The president's lounge. This is used for welcoming sponsors during match days.

Left: Along the main passage photographs of Rovers' great players and matches are displayed.

Below: Darren Calow of DC Training gives his Man of the Match award to Paul Green in the president's lounge after the Margate game of the 2002/03 season.

The view from the home team's changing rooms. This is what the players see as they enter the field and where many young fans would love to run out wearing Rovers' colours.

The home team's bath which many people would like to try. Now, however, most players prefer the showers.

The view going
up the stairs to
the Main Stand.

The LNER
replica
nameplate for
B17 Doncaster
Rovers.
The original
nameplate was
sold off in the
1990s.

Above: The entrance for the man we love to hate: the door to the referee's room.

Right: A view of the inside of the referee's room with the door to the main passage and the away team's exit to the pitch.

Left: Inside the referee's room showing all the mod cons, and a toilet.

Below: The boardroom after the Manchester United friendly on 27 July 2001 with soon-to-be-director Paul May, and the then-chief executive Joe Hoggins.

Director Trevor Milton and his wife Renee in the boardroom after the Manchester United friendly on 27 August 2001. Trevor Milton was to become chairman and held this position during the club's promotion back into the League.

Bill serves the tea after the Manchester United friendly, August 2001.

The array of trophies and photographs behind the directors' bar in the boardroom.

A display of photographs, framed newspaper cuttings and the pennant given by Manchester United on their visit to Belle Vue in July 2001.

Right: Another view of the boardroom taken from the bar.

Below: The boardroom was changed for the first season back in the Football League with a large walkway knocked out between the VIP lounge and the boardroom to make more space. Both rooms now comprise the boardroom.

The guest/VIP lounge after the friendly match against Manchester United, August 2001. This room is now part of the boardroom and is only for directors and guests.

The bar in the guest lounge with the then-chief executive Joe Hoggins checking all is well before the match against Manchester United, August 2001.

The Executive Club, where players and members met after the game. Behind the bar is Alick Jeffrey Jr, son of Rovers legend Alick Jeffrey. The photograph was taken in August 2001. This area has now been redesigned as another sponsors' lounge.

Waiting for the storm to blow over. Dave Penney and the Rovers players relax in the guest lounge while waiting to start the 2001 photo shoot. The photograph was taken in August 2001.

The new Rovers shop opened during the latter part of the 2000/01 season. This is often the busiest part of the ground on match days and at Christmas.

Tracey Fearnie the shop manager in December 2003.

Rovers with the Community Officer Richard Bailey, in his office hidden away beneath the Main Stand in August 2001. Many community events such as school visits and children's parties are organised by Eric Randerson and Richard from here.

Inside the Rovers community office, which is hidden deep within the Main Stand where no light filters through. This space has been used as a tea room, a storage area and a players' lounge in the past.

The laundry room is one of the essential parts of the Rovers machine, but one which is hardly ever seen. It is here that kit man Dave Richards makes sure that the team are ready for action and wearing the correct kit! The picture was taken in August 2001.

The Rovers first strip drying and awaiting ironing in the laundry room after being worn in a match against Hartlepool United at Gateshead in August 2001.

The players' lounge. This was changed from a sponsors' lounge at the start of the 2003/04 season for use by players.

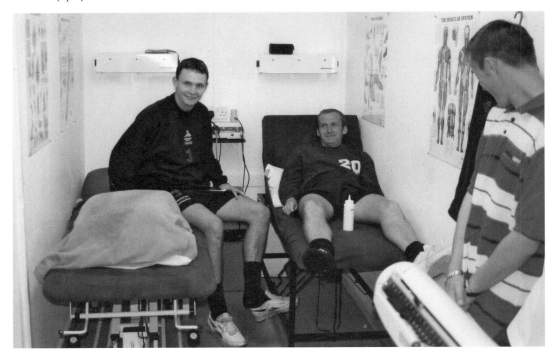

Simon Shaw and Tim Ryan in the physiotherapy room during the early Conference days when Jon Bowden was the club physiotherapist.

The trophy cabinet in the guest bar. Trophies include the Nationwide Conference play-off trophy. The photograph was taken in December 2003.

Barry Watson inside the Supporters' Club office programme section during September 2001.

The Supporters' Club office, in a photograph taken in September 2001.

The away changing rooms. Notice that they are not as comfortable as the home changing rooms and are drearier in appearance.

three

The Main
Stand

Little about the appearance of the Main Stand has changed since it opened in 1922 for the first game against Gainsborough Trinity. The only major change has been the addition of the extended cover at the front, as can be seen by the photograph opposite below. The original 1922 seats were finally removed in December 2003.

During December 2003, the original 1922 seats were finally removed from the Main Stand to make way for new seating. The seats that were recovered were offered to fans in January 2004. Some of the seats still had reserved stickers for season-ticket holders attached to them. When the new executive boxes were built the old seats were destroyed by mistake during clean-up work.

An old 1922 seat. This seat
will have been sat on during the
first match at Belle Vue
in 1922.

Opening day in 1922.

The Main Stand during
the 1970s showing the cover
over the terrace in front of the
seating area.

Not the bridge over the river Kwai, but a bridge allowing fans to gain access to the emergency exit. On the right is the directors' box and the front row where the chairman and guests sit.

A view from the Rossington End in 1985.

A view of the pitch taken from the Main Stand facing towards the Town End.

This is the press box from where all the stories on match day reach the newspapers and radio. The box was enlarged during the first season that the club was back in the Football League. The box is now very often full to the brim with journalists.

Original dugouts shown during a Doncaster Rovers Ladies game in 1999.

The new transparent dugouts for the substitutes and management. These replaced the original brick ones in the summer of 2000.

The tannoy/public address station with the top of the directors'/VIP area in front.

The disabled section of the ground during the game against Yeovil Town, played on Saturday 25 August 2001.

Vandals set light to this roof in the 1980s.

Along the Main Stand Terrace. Notice the vandalised Main Stand roof.

A view from the Main Stand Terrace showing the Town End Stand in the background.

The Main Stand photographed in December during the 2003/04 season.

Above: The Main Stand Terrace photographed during the early 1980s. Notice the absence of barriers compared with today

Right: Stewards get ready before the match against Yeovil on 25 August 2001.

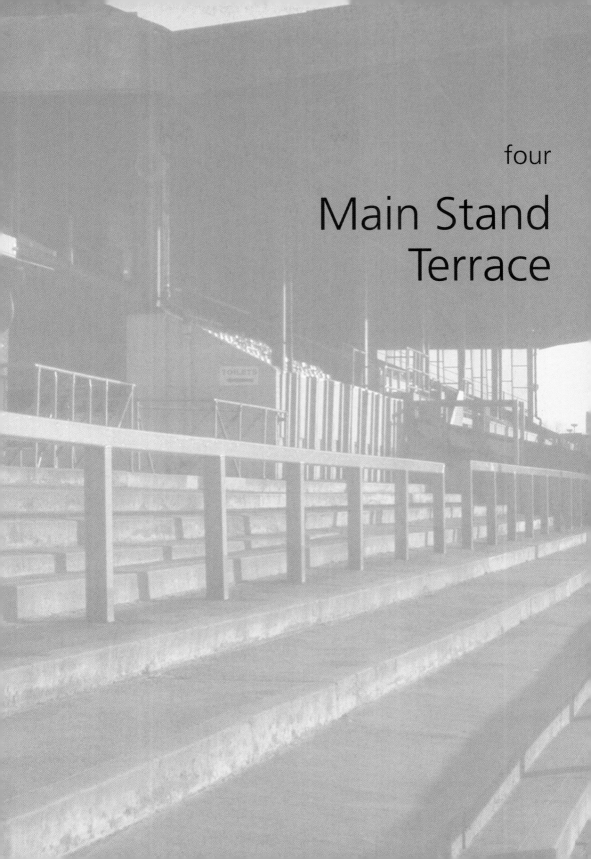

four

Main Stand Terrace

The Main Terrace was built in 1922 in front of the Main Stand and designed to hold 3,000 spectators. With money provided by the Supporters' Club in the summer of 1927, the Main Stand was extended. In 1989, following the Hillsborough Disaster, the capacity was reduced to 2,125. In 1997 the stand was completely reconcreted and new crush barriers were installed.

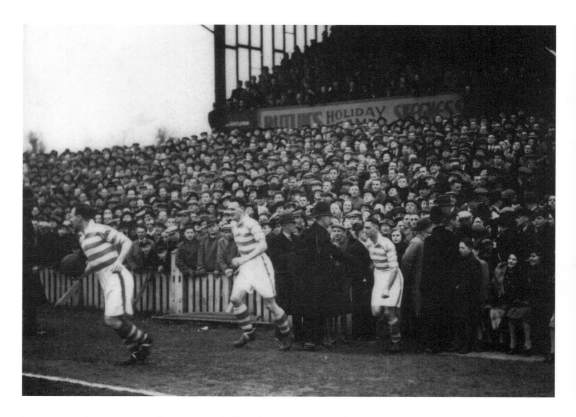

Players running out of the home tunnel. The photograph was taken sometime in the 1930s.

The Town End exit from the Main Stand Terrace onto a very wet car park. This was taken on 9 December 2003.

The Main Stand Terrace, December 2003.

The Main Stand Terrace, all prim and proper before the season starts in August 2001.

The programme sales hut, located at the Town End of the terrace, August 2001.

Ready for a hot pie? The snack bar at the Rossington End of the Main Stand Terrace during the game against Woking, 8 September 2001.

five

Popular
Terrace

Originally the spectators stood on ash banking with no cover, but in 1924 a shelter was added. This was extended in the summer of 1927 along with the Main Stand at a cost of £1,500 which was provided by the Supporters' Club. A year later the Supporters' Club again donated the funds to concrete the Popular Side. In the summer of 1937, with funds supplied by the Supporters' Club, the Popular Side was concreted again. A year later the Popular Side shelter was taken down in order for it to be built further back and raised higher. This extension was concreted and the capacity of the ground was raised to 40,000. In the summer of 1939 the club built a concrete wall the full length of the Popular Side and also laid down a running track for the players.

In May 1987 it was discovered that this side had been hit by mining subsidence. It was subsequently closed, the cover taken down and the top third of the terracing removed. After being reconcreted it was opened as an uncovered terrace. However, in 1989, a ninety-yard-long cover was built at a cost of £50,000.

The Popular Terrace with original roof as it looked in the 1970s.

A view along the Popular Terrace taken after a game in May 2001.

The old Popular Stand, seen from the Town End. This shows the contrast between the Popular Stand and the Rossington End. This was photographed in the 1970s.

The operator's view from inside the Popular Side turnstiles.

The snack bar at the Town End of the Popular Terrace.

A view of the snack bar at the Rossington End of Popular Terrace, all closed up after a game in May 2001.

The Popular Stand in the process of demolition because of subsidence in summer 1987.

A photograph recording the demolition of the original Popular Stand in August 1987.

Desolate and forlorn. This is all that remains of the original Popular Terrace which lies behind the current Popular Stand. This was photographed in winter 2003.

Winter 2003. The terracing and even the collapsed old toilets remain, but are now grassed over.

Above: A view along the Popular Terrace from the Rossington End, December 2003.

Left: Looking down onto the turnstiles at the Town End.

No queues today. The turnstiles to the Popular Stand in December 2003.

The Popular Side in the wake of the demolition of the cover.

six

On the
Pitch

The pitch was built over a bed of ash brought in by the lorry load and has always been known as a very quick-draining ground. It was also the biggest pitch in the country, measuring 119 yards by 79 yards. In 1980, Billy Bremner, the then manager, had the size reduced to 110 yards by 77 yards because he thought opposition teams had far to much space to play their brand of football when they came to play at Belle Vue. It also cut down the amount of running that his own team had to do.

The pitch has always been kept in good condition – so much so that the Wembley Stadium authorities wanted to take the turf to put down at Wembley in the 1970s. In the 2002/03 season, groundsman Peter White won the Nationwide Conference Groundsman of the Year award.

The pitch on a frosty December morning in 2003.

Ball boys getting ready before a match during the 2000/01 season.

A view from the directors' box of players running onto the pitch during the 2000/01 season.

Left and below: The groundsman, Peter White, puts heaters and covers over the Rossington End's goalmouth, winter 2001.

The pitch covered with snow in late winter 2001.

A rather boggy pitch after a rugby game played the previous day. This was photographed in spring 2001.

Mickey Walker and his youth team help prepare the ground for a match after heavy snow in January 2001.

The Silver Eagles Display Team drop in with the match ball before the first home game against Leigh RMI in the 2001/02 season. This was photographed on 21 August 2001.

seven

The Rossington End

The Rossington End, also known as the Spion Kop, was originally a massive bank of ash which the spectators had to stand on. In the summer of 1928, the Supporters' Club provided the funds to concrete the Kop along with the Popular Side. Eventually the Kop was built-up quite steeply and consisted of sixty-two steps of terracing that gave a bird's-eye view of the ground. In the 1970s the top third was sliced off the Kop and a five-a-side, all-weather pitch was built. Later this side, assigned for away supporters, was penned in by metal fencing along half its length from the Main Stand Terrace side. In 1988 this pen was extended to cater for 2,000 visiting supporters at a cost of £50,000 which was funded by the Football Trust. Following the Hillsborough Disaster in April 1989, the capacity of this area was cut to 1,700. In 2003 the Rossington End was extended to cater for larger numbers of visiting away fans after Rovers' promotion back into the Football League.

The Spion Kop during the 1970s.

The Spion Kop of the ground at the first home game of the 1950/51 season.

The same view of the Spion Kop as it was in 2002. It is now much smaller and does not extend back as far.

The five-a-side pitch at the back of the Rossington End in winter 2003. The original Spion Kop covered this area. Rovers in the Community now use this area for parties and school children use the space as their own football ground.

Along the Rossington End before the start of the 2001 season.

The floodlights at the Rossington End, 1965.

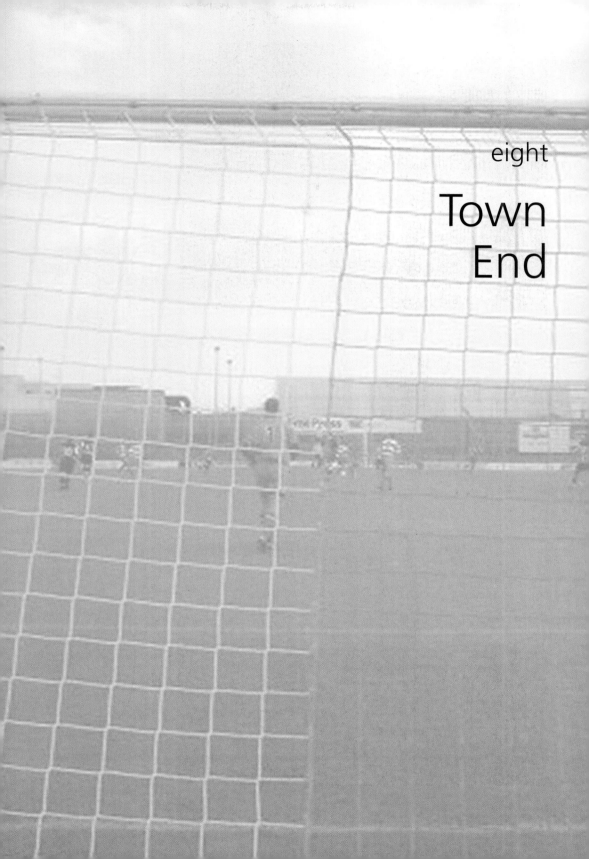

eight

Town
End

In the summer of 1927 the Main Stand on the Bennetthorpe ground, which the Rovers had built during their tenancy from 1920 to 1922, was physically moved down the road to Belle Vue and placed at the Town End of the ground. In order to move the stand, jacks were used and rollers placed underneath, enabling the stand to be hauled into its new resting place. This stand seated around 700 spectators.

In the summer of 1985, in the aftermath of the Bradford fire, this stand was demolished. During the following summer, extensive repair work to the terracing at this end was carried out by the Junior Rovers with concrete donated free of charge by a local firm. Following the Hillsborough Disaster in April 1989, the standing capacity was cut to 510 on this side. In the early 1990s this end of the ground was allowed to slip into disrepair and was eventually closed to the public.

In the summer of 2003 the Town End terracing was concreted for use by home supporters. Then, in the 2004 close season, executive boxes were built at the back of this terracing to bring some much needed revenue into the club.

The Town End Stand in the 1970s. Note the old brick-built dugout on the right.

The Town End
Stand, photographed
in the 1980s.

Grass grows where
supporters' feet once
stood. This area has
now disappeared
after rebuilding
work was started in
summer 2003.

The view along the deserted barriers at the Town End during the summer of 2001.

An overgrown Town End during the 1990s, photographed when the club was in serious decline.

The original
entry steps to
the Town End.

A view from
behind the
Town End,
often known as
'Steptoe's'. This
was taken in
the summer of
2003 before the
rebuilding of the
Town End.

A view of the
Main Stand
from a rather
overgrown Town
End.

Looking through
the net from the
Town End.

Rebuilding the
Town End.

Work was
carried out in
order to make
it safe.

The Town End prior to resurfacing during the 2001/02 season, so it could be reopened in part.

Ready for resurfacing.

Above: The Town End finished.

Left: Fans are back on the Town End for the Dagenham game in September 2002.

The fans are
back.

The lottery
caravan at the
back of the
Town End
during the 1980s.

nine

Offices and the Viking Social Club

During the 2001/02 season it was decided to build a social club to allow the fans to have a drink before the game. The only place available was at the Rossington End of the car park where a portable cabin was installed and a club opened. The club is open before and after games and is also open for the Dragons' matches on Sundays.

Prior to the fire caused by the then chairman Ken Richardson, many of the offices were actually within the Main Stand. After the fire and throughout the Conference years, the offices were moved into portable cabins attached to the Main Stand. The only office that is still within the stand is the accountant's office, which is in the old Supporters' Club room.

Outside the offices.

The club secretary's office with secretary Joan Oldale on the phone. The club's business is conducted here. This photograph was taken in September 2002.

The meeting room in the portable cabins. This is now the media centre, but looks almost the same.

The old portable cabins being moved following the relocation of staff to the new office block in November 2004.

Chairman John Ryan and then-chief executive Joe Hoggins are pictured here visiting the new Viking Social Club on the opening day.

The Viking Social Club is dwarfed by the former floodlight pylon which is now used for telecommunications.

The new office block, with the staff offices and ticket office on the left and the new 'Rovers Return' Social Club on the right.

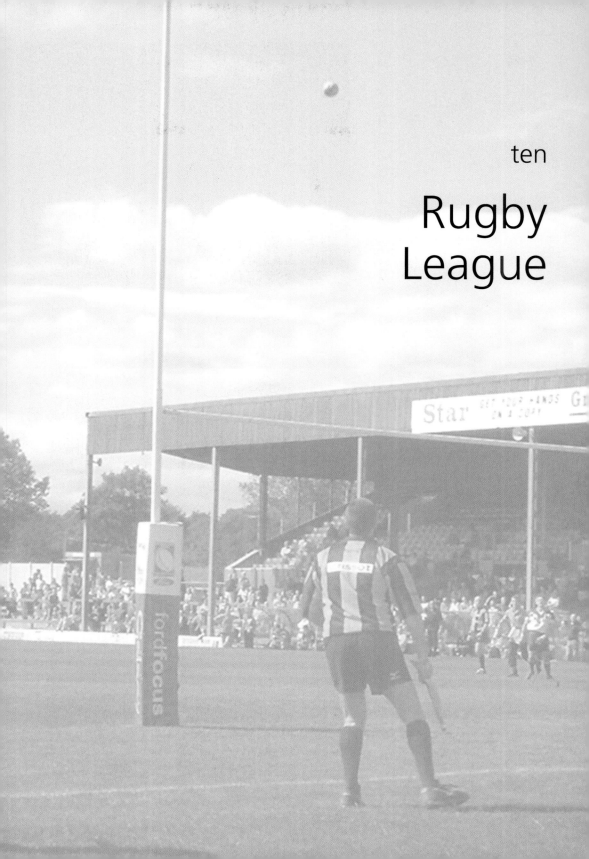

ten

Rugby League

Rugby League was first played at Belle Vue on Tuesday evening, 24 March 1953. This was a match between a Doncaster Past & Present XIII and a Rugby League All Stars XIII played under floodlights. It had been arranged to raise funds for Doncaster Rugby League club, which was in financial trouble.

For the 1995 season the renamed Doncaster Dragons left the Tattersfield Stadium on Bentley Road for the Meadowcourt Greyhound Stadium at Stainforth. In the interim, on 20 August 1995, they played a game at Belle Vue.

In 1998, Stainforth not having proved an ideal venue, the club came to an agreement with Doncaster Rovers to move to Belle Vue. Rugby League was now played on Sundays so there would not be any clashes with the Rovers games. In November 2004 the rugby club staff moved into new offices along with the Rovers staff.

Different posts and an oddly shaped ball make an appearance at Belle Vue.

A whole different crowd look out from the Main Stand on a hot summer day.

Scrum down at Belle Vue.

Setting up the padding for the rugby posts before a game at Belle Vue.

Another view from the Popular Stand picturing a Sunday afternoon's rugby league match.

During the 2002 season the Dragons set up a scoreboard at the Town End, but this has now moved due to the rebuilding work and is now at the Rossington End.

eleven

Sky at
Belle Vue

Saturday 7 September 2002 saw the first live broadcast of a complete match from Belle Vue. Rovers entertained Dagenham & Redbridge in front of the Sky Television cameras and over 4,000 fans inside the ground. This was a new experience for all at Belle Vue, with gantries, wires and cameras everywhere both inside and outside the ground.

Sky Television lorries parked outside Belle Vue.

Sky Sports cameras overlooking the pitch from their position halfway along the Popular Side.

twelve

Aerial Views
of Belle Vue

Here are two aerial views of Belle Vue taken over the years, showing the changing face not only of the ground, but also of the surrounding area. Unfortunately we have very few original photographs of these particular views, so these pictures have been reproduced using programmes. One photograph which has as yet sadly eluded us, is an aerial photograph taken while a match is being played. Unfortunately, nobody has been able to help us with our search.

The 1949/50 season. Notice the Bennetthorpe Stand on the left.

The ground as it was in 2001. What is noticeable about this photograph is the expanse behind the Rossington End where the original Spion Kop once stood.

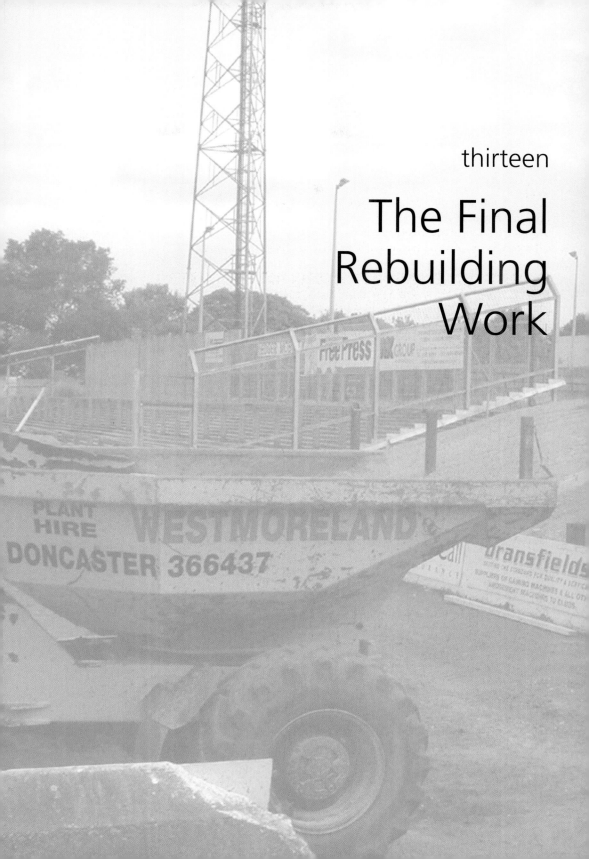

thirteen

The Final Rebuilding Work

The summer of 2003 saw the club enter the Football League once more after five years in the wilderness of the Nationwide Conference. With the club's re-entry into the League and the prospect of larger crowds, the club took the decision to enlarge the ground. This was achieved by expanding the Rossington End for away fans and fully rebuilding the Town End of the grounds. This was completed in time for the first matches back in the Football League to be played and raised the capacity for accommodating spectators from 7,400 to 9,500. However, even with the increased space, the numbers were still well below those of the 1940s and 1950s.

Summer 2003, and dump trucks and diggers move in to take away the remains of the old Town End terrace, where many fans once stood, preparing the area for the new terrace where many will stand for the few years that Belle Vue has remaining before the club move.

All the debris from years of neglect had to be moved before the foundations and cementing could be completed.

The new Town End takes shape.

Work begins on the Rossington End extension.

The grass bank is dug up ready for the cement to be laid for the new Rossington End extension.

The first fans arrive on the new Town End after its complete reconstruction was finished in July 2003.

This is the first game where the extension to the Rossington End was used in August 2003.

Rovers added executive boxes to the Town End to give corporate supporters the chance of watching in style. These were erected during pre-season and were opened for the first game of the 2004/05 season.

In November 2000, Rovers legend Alick Jeffrey, who was probably the most famous player to have graced Belle Vue, died. His funeral took place at Belle Vue and fans laid floral tributes at the Town End. One fan pinned this scarf onto the wooden backboards. The scarf was left there – no one was prepared to take it down until the beginning of the reconstruction started on the Town End in July 2003.

Epilogue

In December 2006, Doncaster's Belle Vue ceased to be the home of the Rovers after eighty-four years of football. It was when I joined the club in 1999 and met up with Tony Bluff that I realised that we could not let the ground disappear without a record of its existence. At that point I started recording every nook and cranny around the old stadium, to make sure that future generations would remember the days when over 20,000 fans walked to the ground to watch the Rovers play in the old Football League Second Division. There have been many books about the club and the players but no one has ever recorded the ground and published it. This is the first Doncaster Rovers official pictorial history of Belle Vue.

Unfortunately photos of Belle Vue are rare, as usually the ground features only as an incidental backdrop to the matches played there. Many of the photos in this book have never been published anywhere else, or have been long forgotten.

Other titles published by Stadia

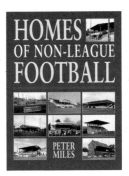

Homes of Non-League Football
PETER MILES

This book catalogues, in words and pictures, the 350 biggest, best-loved, most historically important and beautiful non-League grounds. Compiled by a renowned stadium expert and respected ground photographer over a twenty-five-year period of football travel, it includes vital statistics for every ground and a written account of the clubs and their stadiums.
978 0 7524 2723 2

Doncaster Rovers Football Club
PETER TUFFREY

This collection of nearly 200 photographs, many of which have been taken from private collections as well as the club's own archive, offers a fascinating insight into Rovers' history. Player portraits, team groups, action shots and rare handbook and programme covers, with accompanying text by Rovers expert Peter Tuffrey, tell the story of a club with a quite unique history. It is bound to delight Doncaster Rovers fans everywhere.
978 0 7524 2189 6

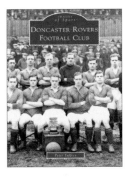

Doncaster Rovers Football Club 100 Greats
PETER TUFFREY

Featuring players from each decade, starting with the 1920s, this book celebrates some of the great footballers who have graced the Belle Vue turf over the years. From Sammy Cowan and Tom Keetley through to Darren Moore, Mark Rankine and Rufus Brevett, it includes players from championship-winning sides and from the non-League years alike. It is sure to stimulate lively debate among Rovers fans.
978 0 7524 2707 2

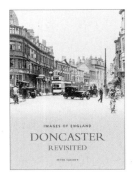

Doncaster Revisited
PETER TUFFREY

This book charts the development of Doncaster from the 1870s to the mid-1990s, with some rare photographs illustrating the great changes that have taken place in the town. Amongst the 200 images are views of St Sepulchre Gate, Market Place and High Street. This book is sure to appeal to anyone who has an interest in the history of Doncaster.
978 0 7524 3233 5

If you are interested in purchasing other books published by Stadia, or in case you have difficulty finding any Stadia books in your local bookshop, you can also place orders directly through the Tempus Publishing website
www.tempus-publishing.com